Saving Our World

RECYCLING
WASTE

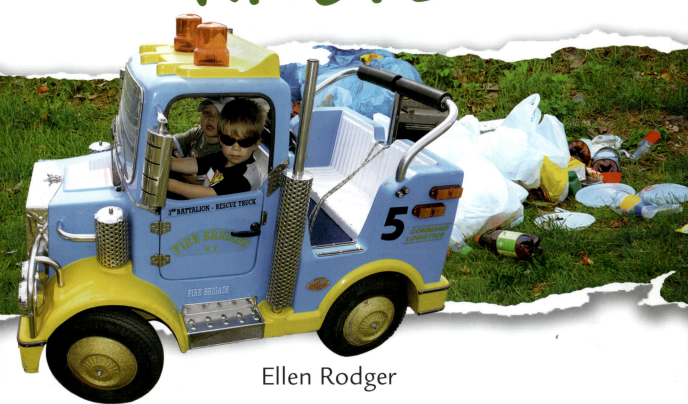

Ellen Rodger

mc **Marshall Cavendish**
Benchmark
New York

Marshall Cavendish Benchmark
99 White Plains Road
Tarrytown, NY 10591
www.marshallcavendish.us

All Internet addresses were available and accurate when this book was sent to press.

Library of Congress Cataloging-in-Publication Data
Rodger, Ellen.
    Recycling waste / by Ellen Rodger.
     p. cm. -- (Saving our world)
    Includes bibliographical references and index.
    ISBN 978-0-7614-3222-7
  1. Refuse and refuse disposal--Juvenile literature.
  2. Recycling (waste, etc.)--Juvenile literature. I. Title.
    TD792.R64 2008
    363.72'82--dc22
    2008014554

The photographs in this book are used by permission and through the courtesy of:

Half Title: Hugo de Wolf/ Shutterstock; maxstockphoto/ Shutterstock

Julien Leblay/ Fotolia: 4-5, maxstockphoto/ Shutterstock: 7, ROBERT BROOK/ Science Photo Library/ Photolibrary: 8-9, Photo Network / Alamy: 10-11, Paul Cowan/ Istockphoto: 12-13, Getty Images: 14-15, ASSOCIATED PRESS: 16-17, Greg Vaughn/Pacific Stock/ Photolibrary: 18-19, Soph / Dreamstime: 20-21, Pixelprof/ Istockphoto: 22-23, Hugo de Wolf/ Shutterstock: 24-25, HP_photo/ Shutterstock: 25, PhillDanze/ Istockphoto: 26-27, SHOUT / Alamy: 28-29,

Cover photo: John Keith Photography/ Istockphoto; Terraxplorer/ Istockphoto; Oleg Prikhodko/ Istockphoto.

Illustrations: Q2AMedia Art Bank

Created by: Q2A Media

Creative Director: Simmi Sikka

Series Editor: Maura Christopher

Series Art Director: Sudakshina Basu

Series Designers: Dibakar Acharjee, Joita Das, Mansi Mittal, Rati Mathur and Shruti Bahl

Series Illustrator: Abhideep Jha and Ajay Sharma

Photo research by Sejal Sehgal

Series Project Managers: Ravneet Kaur and Shekhar Kapur

Printed in Malaysia

1 3 5 6 4 2

CONTENTS

What Is Waste?   4

How Much Trash?   6

What Happens?   8

The Three Rs   10

Why Recycle?   14

Recycling Saves Energy   16

Paper Recycling   18

Glass Recycling   20

Metal Recycling   22

Plastic Recycling   24

Composting Waste   26

Trash the Toaster?   28

Glossary   30

Where to Find Out More   31

Index   32

What Is Waste?

People are trash machines. They create garbage every day simply by living. Many of the products people make, use, and eat create waste that must be sent to garbage dumps or landfill sites.

Ancient Trash

Trash is a fact of life. Even the earliest people on Earth had to deal with trash. One **civilization** that began around the banks of the Indus River, in what is now Pakistan, had an advanced form of trash disposal. The Harappan people who lived there built homes with **garbage chutes**. Trash from the chutes was collected and buried in dumps outside of the city or burned. The Harappans knew that if their trash piled up, their cities could not grow and stay disease-free.

PAKISTAN

Harappa

Indus Plain

Indus River

INDIA

Arabian Sea

Bay of Bengal

The Indus River civilization existed from 3300 BCE to 1700 BCE. Today, scientists are impressed by the sewers and trash collections in cities such as Harappa.

Dealing with Trash

Today, people either dump, burn, or recycle their trash, much as they did in ancient times. The difference between trash in the ancient world and trash today is the amount and the type. Ancient peoples did not have plastic. They wasted less and reused things more. Ancient garbage included food **waste** such as bones, and natural materials such as cotton and leather. These items **decompose**, or rot, more quickly than many items in modern landfills.

> **Waste** *is something that has been thrown out because it is no longer of use. If people recycled and reused more household trash, there would be less waste in landfills.*

QUESTION TIME ❓

Is it dangerous to let trash pile up?

If left to sit, garbage can really stink. This is because a lot of trash is made of matter that comes from living organisms. These **organic** materials decompose over time and can attract pests such as rats, who feed on the trash. Rats often carry diseases, which can be passed to humans. Piled-up trash can also leak chemicals such as bleach from bleach containers.

How Much Trash?

People in the United States create more than 4 pounds of trash per day, or 200 million tons of trash each year. That is enough trash to cover 100,000 football fields in 6 feet of smelly trash!

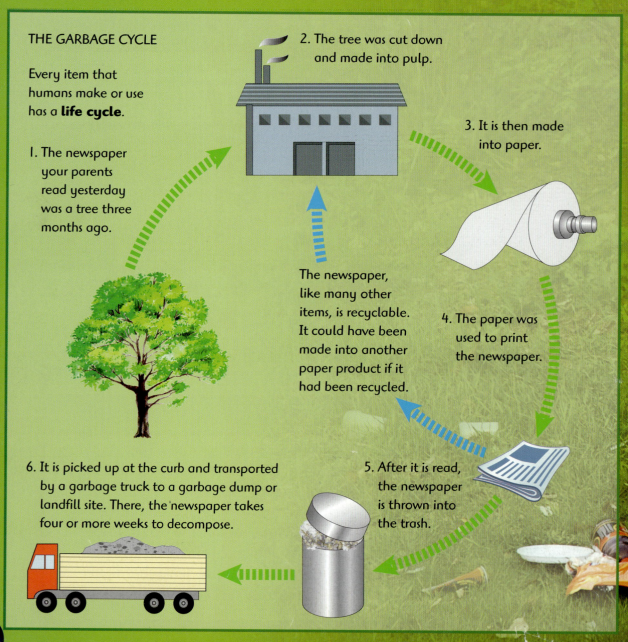

THE GARBAGE CYCLE

Every item that humans make or use has a **life cycle**.

1. The newspaper your parents read yesterday was a tree three months ago.

2. The tree was cut down and made into pulp.

3. It is then made into paper.

The newspaper, like many other items, is recyclable. It could have been made into another paper product if it had been recycled.

4. The paper was used to print the newspaper.

5. After it is read, the newspaper is thrown into the trash.

6. It is picked up at the curb and transported by a garbage truck to a garbage dump or landfill site. There, the newspaper takes four or more weeks to decompose.

Heaps of Trash

Landfills are only temporary solutions to the trash problem. There is only so much land that can be used for dumping. Landfills are usually located away from where people live. In some cities, there is no land left to dump trash. Trucks filled with trash drive hundreds of miles to the nearest dump, which wastes money and fuel energy.

EYE-OPENER

Some trash is burned, or incinerated. Some waste **incinerators** even create energy for electricity through trash burning. Incinerators burn trash that has been sorted into organic material that comes from living things, and **inorganic**, or nonliving, materials. Organic materials include food scraps and substances such as wood, leather, and wool. Inorganic materials include plastics, aluminum, and metals. Incinerators are used in places where land for dumps is scarce, such as in Japan.

Some trash, such as dirty disposable plastic diapers, can take up to five hundred years to biodegrade, or decompose into the environment.

What Happens?

Nobody wants to live next to a landfill. They are not pretty and they attract flocks of scavenging birds. Yet landfills are a fact of life, and many are filling up quickly.

Off to the Dump

Landfills are places where trash is stored and carefully managed away from cities. Before garbage is brought to a landfill, the landfill is prepared with a plastic or clay liner. The liner keeps the trash separate from the surrounding environment. This way, harmful materials in the trash do not damage the soil or any nearby water. Trash in a landfill is kept as dry as possible. Bulldozers cover the trash with soil every day. Trash in a landfill site does not decompose easily. Some items in landfill sites, such as Styrofoam cups, are not **biodegradable** and last for thousands of years.

When landfills fill up with trash, they are closed. Over time, the land may be used again for buildings, housing, and even parks. Landfills must follow guidelines for pollution control so that the land is not toxic.

When waste decays in a landfill, it creates an explosive gas called methane. Methane can be used as an **alternative energy** source to generate electricity. Most large landfills have methane collection systems where wells are drilled into the landfills and the gas is collected in a pipeline. The gas can be **refined** and burned for energy.

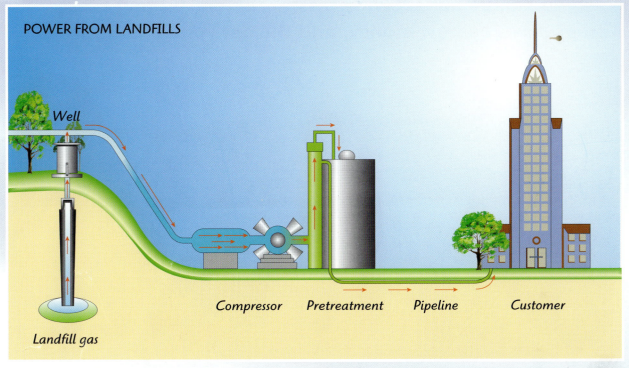

POWER FROM LANDFILLS

Well

Landfill gas

Compressor   Pretreatment   Pipeline   Customer

Before methane gas can be turned into power, it must pass through an air compressor, which controls the flow of the gas, and pretreatment, which cleans it.

Overflowing Piles

Landfills are not meant to last forever. Imagine storing all the things you throw out each year in your backyard. If you were not careful about what you threw out, your backyard would soon be overflowing with waste!

The Three Rs

Each year Americans throw away more and more trash. Reducing, reusing, and recycling trash is the smartest way to handle our growing trash problem. Taking these steps saves energy, money, and the environment.

Garbage

Glass

Paper

The Three Rs

Reducing, reusing, and recycling are called the three Rs so that they are easy to remember. Reducing means buying less and throwing away less. One of the best ways to cut down on the trash sent to landfills is to reduce the amount of trash that is made. This means not buying products that you don't need, such as a new pair of jeans when you have a drawerful. Also avoid buying products that are heavily wrapped or packaged.

The three Rs ask us to give up or reduce doing some of the things we enjoy, such as taking weekly trips to fast-food restaurants that serve food in disposable containers.

Sealed, Boxed, and Wrapped

Have you ever bought something that was wrapped in several layers of plastic, paper, or cardboard? Did you throw away the packaging as soon as you opened the product? Reducing waste requires you to buy smart. Buying smart means questioning whether you really want something with wasteful packaging that will add to the garbage problem. If everyone bought smart, **manufacturers** would have to start packaging products with less plastic, and with more recycled and recyclable material.

QUESTION TIME

Are there rules for reducing trash?

There are no official rules for reducing the amount of trash you create, but there are some things you can do:
- Do not buy things you do not really need.
- Do not buy items that were made to be thrown away, such as disposable batteries.
- Try not to eat in restaurants that serve food in disposable containers.
- Avoid buying cheap things that cannot be repaired.

Reusing Things

Reusing items is another great way you can cut down on trash. Many things can be reused. For instance, you could use an egg carton to hold paper clips and staples. Other reusable items include books, toys, appliances, and furniture. These things can be given away, traded, or sold to other people when you no longer want them.

Styrofoam containers never decompose or break down in a landfill. Luckily, Styrofoam can be recycled into new plastic products.

Recycling

Recycling is a process that turns one manufactured product, such as paper or glass, into another product, such as new paper or new glass. Recycling includes buying and using products made from recycled materials.

What Can Be Recycled?

Many materials can be recycled, including cardboard, aluminum, plastic, and steel. These materials include products such as plastic bags, cereal boxes, ketchup containers, soda bottles, and aluminum foil. It is easy to tell if a product is recyclable. Just look for a recycling symbol on the product's container. Products made from recycled materials are also often clearly marked.

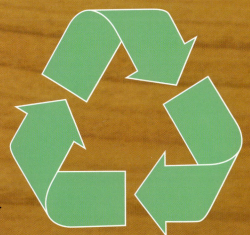

Look for this recycling symbol when you shop.

Why Recycle?

Recycling is not a perfect solution for waste, but it is better than creating more trash and using more of the earth's resources. It is also one step toward green living.

Being Green

Green living means doing whatever you can not to make more waste, create pollution, or use too much energy. Reducing, reusing, and recycling are at the core of green living. Reducing waste and recycling also saves natural resources. These include metals and minerals such as copper, nickel, tin, and iron ore. The mining of these materials creates waste and pollution.

At recycling plants, workers separate plastics, metals, glass, and paper into different "streams." Each stream takes the waste on a different conveyor belt to a separate part of the recycling plant. There it will be remade into reusable plastic, metal, glass, or paper.

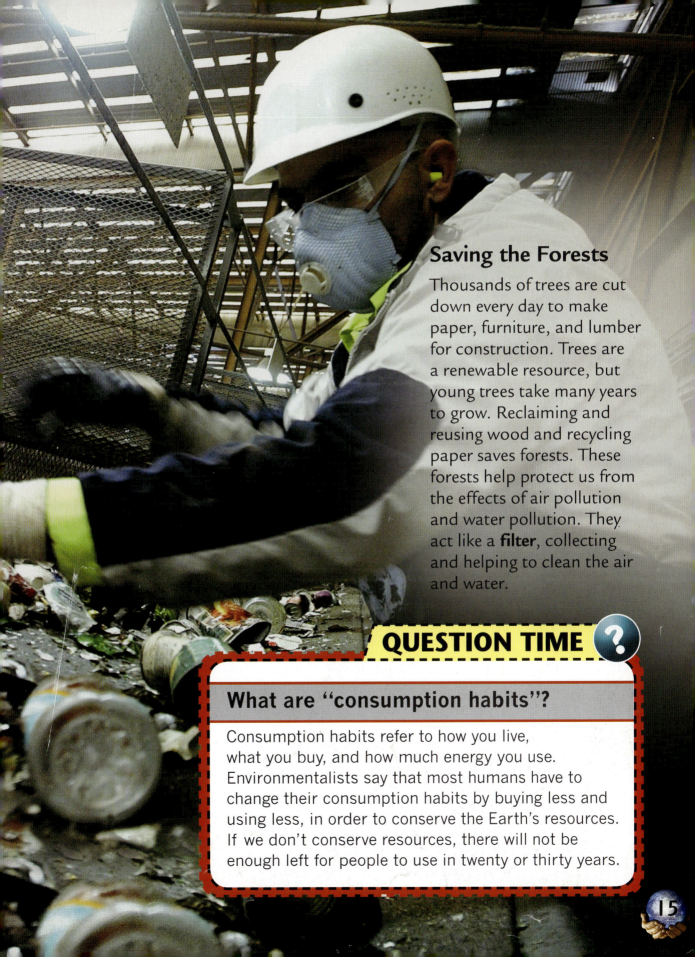

Saving the Forests

Thousands of trees are cut down every day to make paper, furniture, and lumber for construction. Trees are a renewable resource, but young trees take many years to grow. Reclaiming and reusing wood and recycling paper saves forests. These forests help protect us from the effects of air pollution and water pollution. They act like a **filter**, collecting and helping to clean the air and water.

QUESTION TIME ?

What are "consumption habits"?

Consumption habits refer to how you live, what you buy, and how much energy you use. Environmentalists say that most humans have to change their consumption habits by buying less and using less, in order to conserve the Earth's resources. If we don't conserve resources, there will not be enough left for people to use in twenty or thirty years.

Recycling Saves Energy

Recycling is one way to save, or conserve, energy. That's because it takes energy to make new products. It takes much less energy to make similar products using recycled materials.

Want fries with that? Some people reuse cooking oil to power their cars. This saves money and the environment.

Why Save Energy?

Almost everything we make or use today requires energy from fossil fuels such as oil, coal, and natural gas. Unfortunately, fossil fuels pollute when they are burned for energy. Fossil fuels are also nonrenewable. Once they are used, they are gone. Scientists estimate that the world's known supply of oil will run out in forty to fifty years. The world's coal supplies should last 150 years. Dwindling supplies of fossil fuels and pollution are two reasons we should save energy.

Recycling and Energy Use

Recycling is a smart way to save energy. Plastic is a material made from **petrochemicals**, which in turn are made from oil and gas. When plastics are recycled and used again, less oil and gas is used. It takes energy to transport, sort, and process recyclable material, but it takes much less than the amount of energy used to make an entirely new product. Making a new aluminum can, for example, requires an enormous amount of energy in the form of gasoline and electricity. Energy is needed to mine the raw materials and transport, process, and manufacture the can.

EYE-OPENER

When fossil fuels are burned to make products, they emit gases. These gases trap the Sun's heat in Earth's **atmosphere,** gradually warming the planet. Recycling cuts the amount of these gases. This helps protect Earth from **global warming**.

Paper Recycling

Paper is made from trees. Trees must continually be replanted in order to make more paper. Recycling paper conserves forests and saves landfill space.

Home, Office, and School

More than half of the paper used today in the United States is made from recycled paper. That paper comes from homes, schools, industries, and offices across the country. Paper recycling is easy. More than 80 percent of the country has access to a paper-recycling program.

QUESTION TIME ?

How is paper recycled?

Paper collected for recycling is sent to recycling centers where staples and paperclips are removed. The paper is then baled, or wrapped in a large package, and sent to a mill where it is shredded and mixed with water to make a mash of fibers called pulp. The pulp is washed and made into a slush. The slush is mixed with coatings or dyes and is squeezed against a screen to get rid of the water. It is then flattened with rollers to become paper. The paper is dried and rolled into massive spools, ready to be used.

In tropical areas of the world, paper is made from bamboo. Bamboo is a fast-growing plant with a woody stem. It is sturdy and can replace trees in paper-making.

Reuse and Save

Recycling paper is not the only way to save forests. Using and reusing paper wisely also cuts down on the amount wasted. You and your family can cut down on paper use by not printing out everything from the computer, using both sides of a sheet of paper, and sharing newspapers and magazines with others.

Glass Recycling

Glass is a manufactured product that is used in everything from food jars and bottles to cars and houses. Glass is easy to make and just as easy to recycle.

Making Glass

Glass can be made by nature when volcanic eruptions melt rock. It can also be made by humans. Ancient peoples made glass into decorative beads as far back as 3500 BCE. Glass is made from a mixture of sand, soda ash, and lime from limestone that is heated at a high temperature. Once heated, the mixture becomes liquid and can be formed into panes, or vessels such as bottles and glasses.

Recycling Glass

Glass makes up about 10 percent of household waste. It is one product that can be recycled almost indefinitely. Once it is collected and sorted, glass is crushed into **cullet**. The cullet is mixed with more sand, ash, and lime, heated and made into recycled glass products. These include jewelry and Enviroglass, a countertop and flooring material. Glasphalt, a road building material, is made of 30 percent recycled glass.

Can all glass be recycled?

Light bulbs and glass cookware such as Pyrex should not be recycled. They contain material other than glass. Some recycling programs ask you to sort clear, green, and brown glass bottles. Some also ask you to not recycle glass windowpanes because often the glass is altered and contains unacceptable chemicals.

It takes energy and heat to make glass. Less energy is used to make recycled glass because crushed glass melts at a lower temperature.

Metal Recycling

Steel is the most commonly recycled material in the United States. Most steel is recycled from automobiles and appliances at scrap and salvage yards. Aluminum, another common metal, is recycled through can collections.

It takes almost eight hours of electricity to make enough aluminum for thirty-four aluminum cans. It takes less than an hour of electricity to make the same amount of cans from recycled aluminum.

Manufacturing vs. Recycling

Most soda cans today are made from aluminum, a metal mined from an ore, or rock, called bauxite. Bauxite is refined, or made into aluminum, in a process that uses a lot of electricity. It also takes a lot of energy to mine the bauxite and transport it to the refinery.

The Process

When a used can is tossed into the trash, it sits in a landfill for up to five hundred years before it falls apart. When it is recycled, it is taken to a recycling plant where is it shredded and melted. The molten-hot aluminum is poured into a brick, or ingot, to harden. The hardened ingot is rolled into a sheet, ready to be remade into new cans. Aluminum can be repeatedly recycled, so the process is almost endless. This is an example of **closed-loop recycling**. In closed-loop recycling the process continues again and again, for instance with old cans being recycled into new cans that can be recycled again.

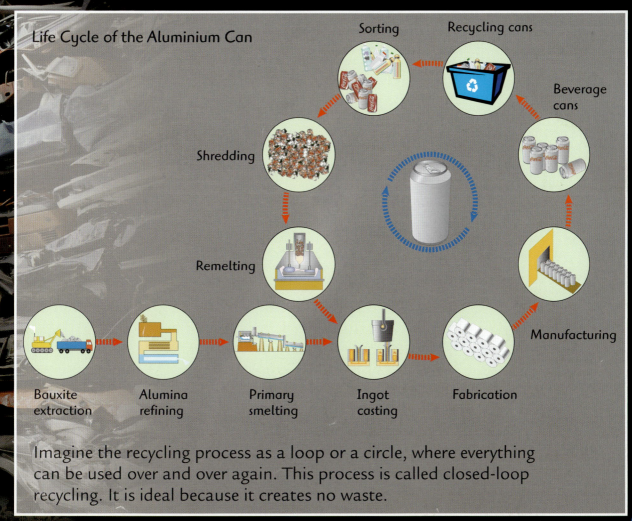

Life Cycle of the Aluminium Can

Sorting

Recycling cans

Beverage cans

Shredding

Remelting

Manufacturing

Bauxite extraction

Alumina refining

Primary smelting

Ingot casting

Fabrication

Imagine the recycling process as a loop or a circle, where everything can be used over and over again. This process is called closed-loop recycling. It is ideal because it creates no waste.

Plastic Recycling

It would be hard to go through a day without using something made from plastic. Everyday items such as toothbrushes, yogurt containers, sneakers, and video game consoles are made of plastic.

Life Before Plastic

Scientists began developing **synthetic** plastics in the late 1800s. It was not until the 1950s that plastic products became common. In 1951, scientists invented polypropylene and polyethylene, the world's most widely used plastics. Today there are ten thousand different kinds of plastic. Almost all plastics today are made from fossil fuels, which are a nonrenewable resource.

Making and Recycling Plastics

Plastics are made by refining petroleum and natural gas into their components, called petrochemicals. The process creates a powder called polymer. Polymer is melted and molded into pellets that can be melted and molded into products. This process uses energy and creates waste. However, plastics can be recycled through different recycling processes, depending on the type of plastic. In all of the processes, plastic is cleaned, melted, and reformed into pellets, ready to be remolded into other products.

Does plastic break down in a landfill?

With enough time, light, and heat, all plastics degrade, or fall apart. But in landfills, trash is covered with a layer of soil, so it is more difficult for light to penetrate. Some plastics made today have additives that speed up **degradation**. There are even biodegradable plastics, which decompose, or rot. They are not great for recycling because most recyclers want plastics that are strong and do not decompose easily.

*Some plastic products, such as this toy fire truck, are made into an entirely new product, such as a fleece jacket, which cannot be recycled again. This one-time-only process is called **open-loop recycling**, or downcycling.*

Composting Waste

Food scraps and the trimmings left over from meals make up a lot of what people put in the trash. Composting scraps and overripe fruits and vegetables is a smart way to cut waste and help the environment.

What Is Compost?

Compost is a pile or container of food, grass trimmings, leaves, and other organic materials that are biodegrading, or rotting. Organic material decomposes easily. When composted, it creates an earthy, nutrient-rich mix. The mix can be used to feed plants and make garden soil fertile.

How to Compost

It is easy to start composting. All you have to do is collect kitchen scraps such as fruit and vegetable peels, crushed eggshells, and even bits of bread. Meat and bones can be composted too, but they are often smelly and attract animals. Scraps can be added to a backyard pile along with grass cuttings. The compost pile, which can be kept in a bin, needs to be turned every so often so that air can help the material rot. After the mix has completely composted, be sure to use it as **fertilizer**! Some recycling programs even collect food scraps. They are brought to a central facility, where the compost is created.

In worm composting, worms consume some of the food waste and create a rich soil through their droppings.

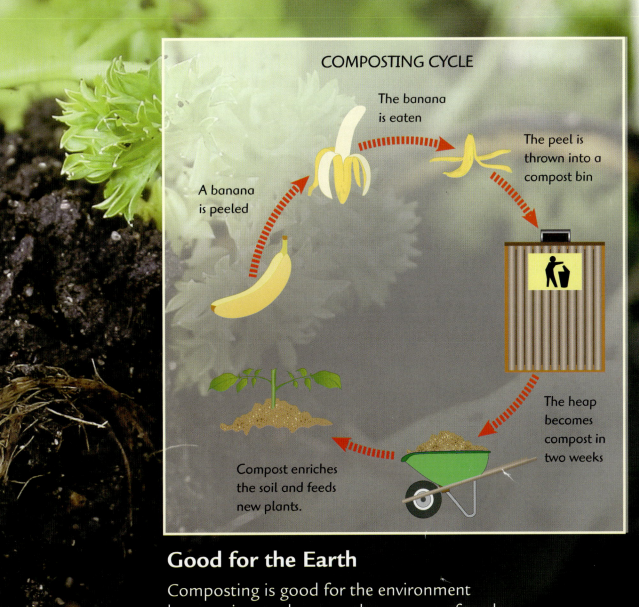

COMPOSTING CYCLE

The banana is eaten

A banana is peeled

The peel is thrown into a compost bin

The heap becomes compost in two weeks

Compost enriches the soil and feeds new plants.

Good for the Earth

Composting is good for the environment because it cuts down on the amount of trash going to landfills. Composting is also a natural process. Everything in nature rots and this helps contribute nutrients to the soil. Scientists believe that if everyone composted, the waste going to landfills would be reduced by 40 to 60 percent.

Trash the Toaster?

Have you ever wondered where your family's old washer and dryer or toaster ends up when it is worn out? Major household appliances are among the easiest to recycle.

Junkyard Recycling

Junk, or salvage, yards may look messy, but most are highly organized recycling facilities. Salvage yards dismantle, or take apart, wrecked cars and appliances. They sell some parts for reuse. Metal is sorted, graded, and sold to steel companies for recycling. Salvage yards separate the electronic parts of vehicles and appliances. They also take the hazardous fluids, such as battery acid and **Freon**, from cars and refrigerators, and dispose of them safely.

More than 70 percent of used televisions, computers, and cell phones in the United States end up in landfills instead of at recycling facilities.

Recycling Computers

An estimated 30 to 40 million personal computers are thrown away each year. This trash is called electronic waste, or **e-waste**. Many older computers, televisions, and other electronic equipment contain lead and other metals that are harmful to the environment. Some recycling companies have equipment that can take the e-waste and separate and shred it into its original materials of plastic, aluminum, steel, metals, and glass without harming the environment. Those materials can then be sold to other recyclers.

EYE-OPENER

Some charities sell the used equipment to **salvagers**. They sell the e-waste in **third-world** countries instead of recycling it. There, people burn the electronics to extract useful metals from wires. Burning the e-waste creates toxic chemicals, which can harm people and the environment. So, before donating e-waste, be smart and ask where it is going and how it will be disposed of.

Glossary

atmosphere: The layers of gases that surround and protect the earth.

alternative energy: A source of energy, or power, that does not come from fossil fuels and is better for the environment.

biodegradable: Can decay, or rot, completely.

civilization: An organized society of people living in a certain place at a certain time.

closed-loop recycling: When a product, such as a used soda can, can be recycled and made into the same product, such as a new soda can, over and over again.

compost: A mixture of decaying organic material used to fertilize plants.

cullet: Crushed glass added to new material to make recycled glass.

decompose: To rot.

degradation: The process of breaking down, or decaying.

e-waste: Electronic waste. Any electric or electronic item that has been thrown out.

fertilizer: A mixture used to make soil rich for growing crops.

filter: Something that separates that traps pollution and lets clean air and water pass through.

Freon: A brand name for a gas used to make refrigerators cold.

garbage chute: A tube or gutter where trash is thrown.

global warming: The increase in the temperature of the Earth's atmosphere.

incinerator: An enormous furnace that burns trash.

inorganic: Nonliving, or something created from materials that are not animal- or plant-based.

life cycle: The cycle of life from birth to death.

manufacturer: A person or company that makes a product.

open-loop recycling: When a product can be recycled and remade into a new product once. Also called *downcycling*.

organic: Made from living things.

petrochemical: A chemical from a natural gas or petroleum.

refine: To purify; or, to bring to another state or product.

salvager: Someone who saves and sells useful materials from old products.

synthetic: Something that is not formed in nature, but by humans through a chemical process.

third world: Countries where most of the population is poor, and where there is little industrial development.

waste: Material that has been used, or is no longer of use, and has been thrown away.

Where to Find Out More

- Information on recycling cell phones:
  www.recyclewirelessphones.com, or
  www.nrc-recycle.org/localresources.aspx

- Electronics recycling information:
  www.eiae.org

- Simple recycling advice:
  www.greenpeace.org

- The National Institute of Environmental Health Sciences Web site
  http://kids.niehs.nih.gov/recycle.htm

- A site that makes knowing how and what to recycle easier:
  http://42explore.com/recycle.htm

- Information on how recycling protects the environment:
  www.epa.gov

- Reuse site: www.freecycle.org

Index

alternative energy, 9

appliance, 12, 22, 28

bauxite, 22, 23

biodegradable, 8, 25

clay liner, 8

coal, 17

compost, 26-27

conserve, 15, 16, 18

consumption, 15

cullet, 20

decompose, 5, 6, 7, 8, 12, 25, 26

degradation, 25

e-waste, 29

Enviroglass, 20

environment, 7, 8, 10, 16, 26, 27, 29

environmentalist, 15

filter, 15

forest, 15, 18, 19

fossil fuel, 17, 24

Freon, 28

garbage, 4, 5, 6, 8, 11

glasphalt, 20

glass, 13, 14, 20-21, 29

global warming, 17

green living, 14

household waste, 20

incinerator, 7

Indus River, 4

inorganic material, 7

Japan, 7

landfill, 4, 5, 6, 7, 8, 9, 11, 12, 18, 23, 25, 27, 28

manufacturer, 11,

methane, 9

natural gas, 17, 24

nonrenewable resource, 17, 24

oil, 16, 17

organic material, 5, 7, 26

paper, 6, 11, 13

petrochemical, 17, 24

petroleum, 24

plastic, 5, 7, 8, 11, 12, 13, 14, 17, 24, 25, 29

pollution, 8, 14, 15, 17

polyethylene, 24

polymer, 24

polypropylene, 24

Pyrex, 21

reclaiming, 15

reduce, 11

refined, 9, 22

refinery, 22

renewable resource, 15

reuse, 5, 12, 16, 19, 28

steel, 13, 22, 28, 29

Styrofoam, 8, 12

United States, 6, 18, 22, 28

zero waste, 13